BEES

Bees have five eyes.
They can see colours
that we can't see.
They see shapes differently, too.
Flowers have special colours
that show bees where to feed.

This is what most people can see.

This is what a bee can see.

FISH

Some fish can see well
in the dark.
It can be very dark
under the water.
Their eyes help them
to find food
in the dark water.

This is what most people can see.

I am a
hammerhead
shark.

This is what some fish can see.

My eyes are on
the side of my head.
How do you think
this helps me?

Take a Look

Contents

Animal
EYES

Written by Sasha Charles

Many animals
do not see things
the same way we do.
Their eyes are different.
Their eyes help them
to find food better.

PENGUINS

Penguins have oil
in their eyes.
The oil acts like sunglasses.
It blocks some
of the blue colour.
This helps penguins
see food better
under the water

This is what most people can see.

How do things change when you wear sunglasses?

This is what a penguin can see.

FROGS

Frogs cannot see
green very well.
They can see blue
much better than green.
If frogs are in danger,
they jump into the water.

Frogs have
two sets of eyelids.
One set is clear.
They are like goggles.
They help frogs see
under the water.

This is what most
people can see.

This is what
a frog can see.

CROCODILES

Crocodiles can't see well when they are cold. They can't catch food when they can't see. So they like to rest in warm places.

This is what a warm crocodile can see.

This is what a cold crocodile can see.

CATS

Cats can see well at night. Their eyes help them hunt in the dark.

Cats are good at seeing things that move. They can't see colours very well.

This is what most people can see.

This is what a cat can see.

PEOPLE

Some people can't see colour very well. Jack is colour blind. Jack can't see green well. Jack's son Jagjeet is not colour blind.

Jack

Jagjeet

This is what Jack can see.

Did you know that more boys than girls are colour blind?

This is what Jagjeet can see.

Zoom In

Written by Kuljit Kaur and Erin Hanifin

Many tools can help us to see up close.
Some tools help us to see faraway things.
Some tools help us to see
very small things.

We can zoom in
with a magnifying glass.

We can zoom in
with a telescope.

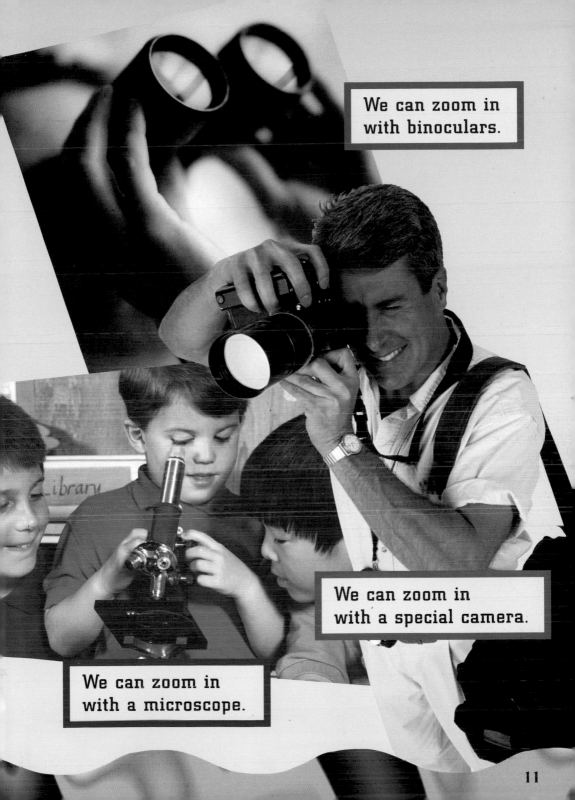

We can zoom in
with binoculars.

We can zoom in
with a special camera.

We can zoom in
with a microscope.

Doctors need to see very small things inside us.
This doctor is using a special tool
to look inside a girl's ear.
He wants to find out why it hurts.

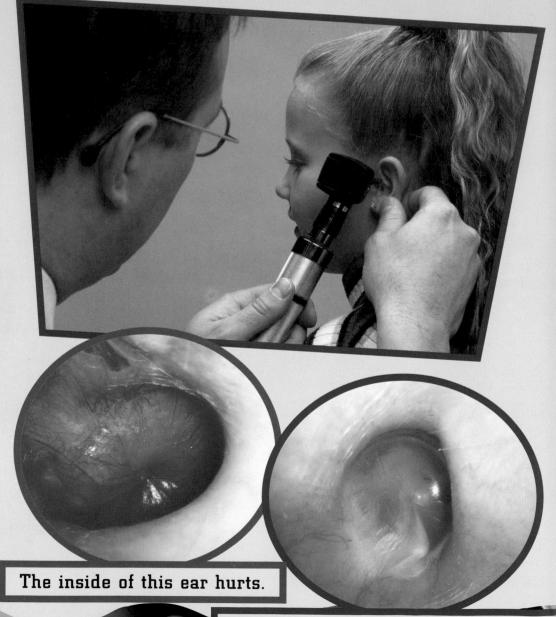

The inside of this ear hurts.

The inside of this ear does not hurt.

Doctors use close-up pictures, too.
Here are some close-up pictures of blood.

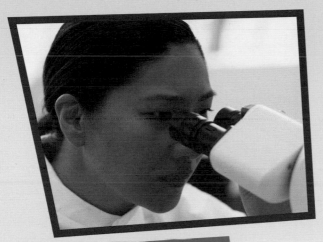

This blood came from
a healthy person.

This blood came
from a sick person.

We can use a special camera
to take close-up pictures of animals.
It is not safe to get close to some animals.
The man in this truck is taking
a picture of a cheetah from far away.

This is what
the man
can see.

The Hubble Space Telescope
took these pictures.
It has taken pictures of places
people have never seen before.
The pictures help us to learn more about space.

What other
tools help us
see up close?

Hubble Space
Telescope

THE Angel

Plane

Written by Erin Hanifin
Illustrated by Marjorie Scott

The next day...

What's wrong with Kamal?

Kamal fell when she was little and hurt her eyes.

The doctors on the Angel Plane will come soon to fix Kamal's eyes.

Ten weeks later...

There are lots of people here, Kamal. They need eye doctors, too.

Are any of them like me? I can only see shapes.

ORBIS

Yes. You can meet them later.

Good, I have lots to ask them.

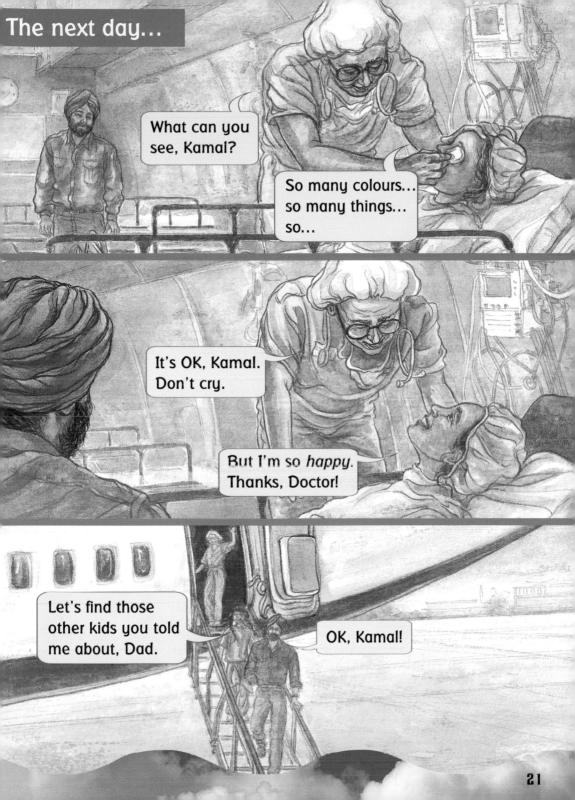

...and the best student prize goes to Kamal!

Thanks, Angel Plane! You helped me to win this.

Thanks for the beautiful pillow, Kamal. How much did Grandma help you?

Lots, because I still can't see the very small shapes.

But you are catching on quickly, Kamal.

Eye TRICKS

Written by Lucy Blake and Kuljit Kaur

Our eyes can play tricks on us.

Sometimes we can see things that are not there.

Sometimes we can't see things that are there.

Try these eye tricks.

Now you see it – now you don't!

Close your left eye.

Hold the picture out as far as you can.

Look at the cross with your right eye.

Slowly bring the picture closer.

What happens to the green dot?

Keep trying until the dot or cross disappears.

Close your right eye.

Look at the green dot as you bring the picture closer. What happens to the cross?

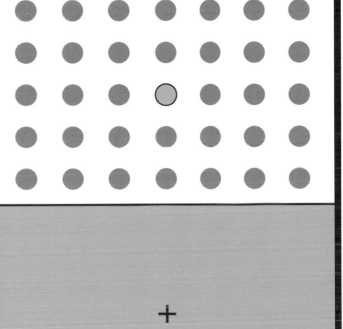

25

Which arrows can you see first?

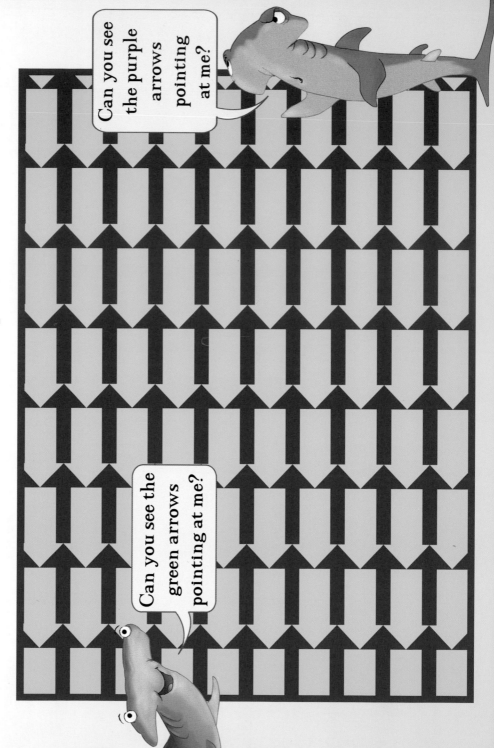

26

Trick your eyes

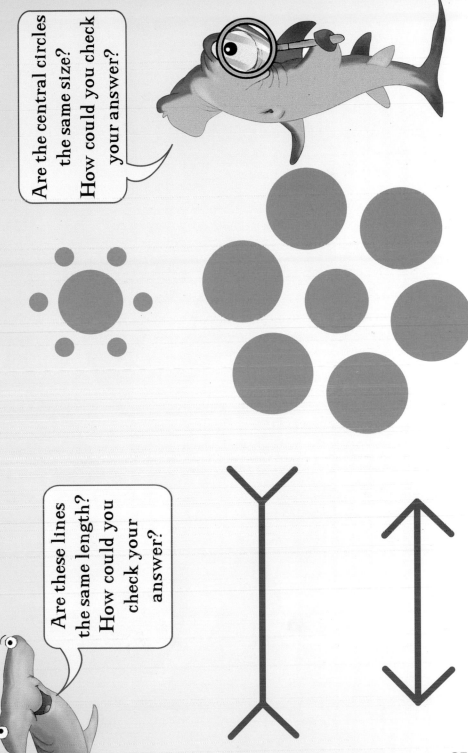

Are the central circles the same size? How could you check your answer?

Are these lines the same length? How could you check your answer?

See with your eyes shut

Look at the dot
in the middle
of the swirl
for a minute.

Then close
your eyes.

What can you
still see?

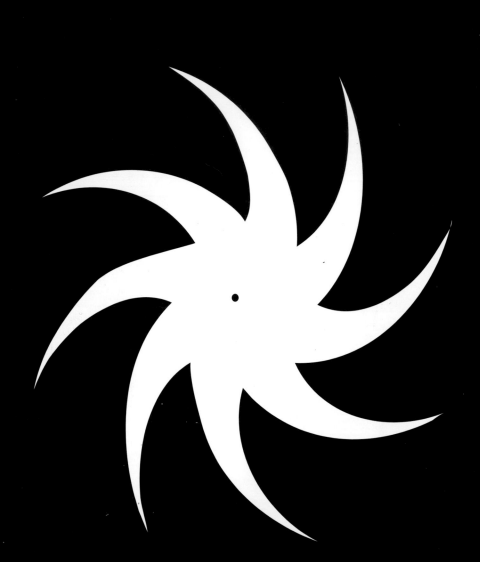

Can you see the fuzzy dots in some of the white spaces?

What happens when you look at one of the dots?

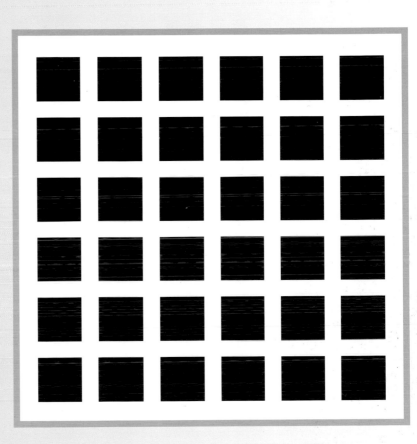

See it move!

What happens to the patterns?

Look around the picture.

30

Be seeing you...

Now that you have done some eye tricks, think about these things:

- Do you see things in the same way all the time?

- Did you find your blind spot?

- How can sizes look different but be the same?

- What other questions do you have about eyes?

Index